Instruments and Music

Brass

Daniel Nunn

www.raintreepublishers.co.uk
Visit our website to find out more information about Raintree books.

To order:
☎ Phone 0845 6044371
🗎 Fax +44 (0) 1865 312263
🖱 Email myorders@raintreepublishers.co.uk

Customers from outside the UK please telephone +44 1865 312262

Raintree is an imprint of Capstone Global Library Limited, a company incorporated in England and Wales having its registered office at 7 Pilgrim Street, London, EC4V 6LB – Registered company number: 6695582

Text © Capstone Global Library Limited 2012
First published in hardback in 2012
The moral rights of the proprietor have been asserted.

Edited by Dan Nunn, Rebecca Rissman, and Sian Smith
Designed by Joanna Hinton-Malivoire
Picture research by Mica Brancic
Production by Victoria Fitzgerald
Originated by Capstone Global Library Ltd
Printed and bound in China by Leo Paper Products Ltd

ISBN 978 1 406 22434 4 (hardback)
15 14 13 12 11
10 9 8 7 6 5 4 3 2 1

British Library Cataloguing in Publication Data
Nunn, Daniel.
   Brass. -- (Instruments and music)
   1. Brass instruments--Juvenile literature.
   I. Title II. Series
   788.9'19-dc22

Acknowledgements
We would like to thank the following for permission to reproduce photographs: Alamy pp.8 (© Lebrecht Music and Arts Photo Library/ Chris Stock), 23 centre (© Lebrecht Music and Arts Photo Library/ Chris Stock), 10 (© imagebroker/Martin Siepmann), 17 (© Lebrecht Music and Arts Photo Library/Odile Noel); © Capstone Publishers pp. 21 (Karon Dubke), 22 (Karon Dubke); Getty Images pp. 13 (Hulton Archive/Frank Pocklington/Stringer), 14 (Robert Harding World Imagery/Maurice Joseph), 18 (AFP/Narinder Nanu), 20 (Stone/ Tony Page); iStockphoto.com pp. 5 centre left (© DNY59), 5 top right (© Goktugg), 5 bottom left (© RodrigoBlanco), 5 bottom right (© RodrigoBlanco), 5 top left (© RodrigoBlanco), 9 (© Cagri Oner); Photolibrary pp. 4 (Radius Images), 7 (age fotostock/Josu Altzelai), 11 (Moodboard), 15 (Dallas & John Heaton), 16 (Japan Travel Bureau), 19 (Corbis), 23 bottom (age fotostock/Josu Altzelai), 23 top (Tetra Images/ Rob Lewine); Shutterstock pp. 6 (© Leon Ritter), 12 (© mountainpix).

Cover photograph of a band of tuba musicians in Macau, China, reproduced with permission of Getty Images (Lonely Planet Images/ Richard I'Anson). Back cover photograph of a tuba player reproduced with permission of iStockphoto.com (© Cagri Oner).

We would like to thank Jenny Johnson, Nancy Harris, Dee Reid, and Diana Bentley for their assistance in the preparation of this book.

Every effort has been made to contact copyright holders of material reproduced in this book. Any such omissions will be rectified in subsequent printings if notice is given to the publisher.

Contents

Brass instruments

trumpet

clarinet

People play many instruments to make music.

People blow brass instruments.

Not all brass instruments are made
of brass.

mouthpiece

People play by making their
lips buzz into a mouthpiece.

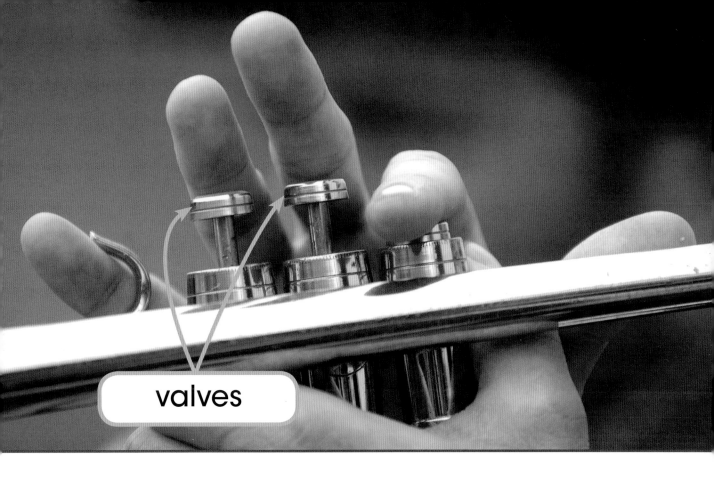

valves

People play notes by pressing keys called valves.

Different brass instruments

A piccolo trumpet is small.

It plays high notes.

A tuba is very big.

It plays low notes.

A sousaphone wraps around the
person playing it.

sliding tube

A trombone has a sliding tube.

Unusual brass instruments

This alphorn is very long.

This tuba is very big.

A conch shell trumpet is made from a seashell.

A didgeridoo is made from the branch of a tree.

Playing brass instruments

Some people play brass instruments outside.

Some people play brass instruments inside.

Some people play brass instruments for work.

Some people play brass instruments just for fun!

Making brass instruments

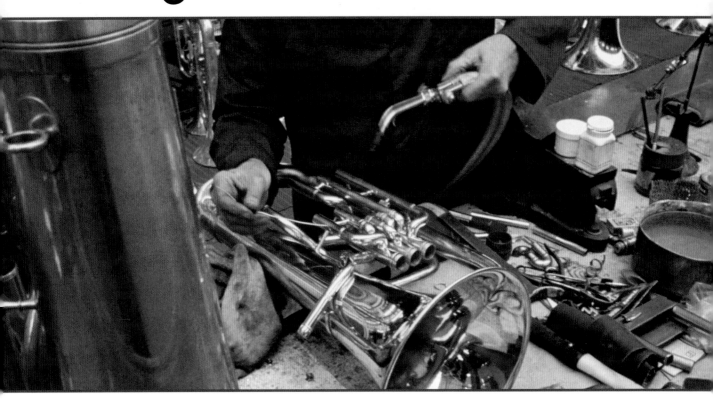

Some brass instruments are hard
to make.

Some brass instruments are easy
to make.

Play your own brass instrument

You can play your own brass instruments, too!

Picture glossary

 **mouthpiece** part of an instrument that you blow into

 **note** sound made by a musical instrument

 **valve** key on a brass instrument that you press to change the note

Index

Notes for parents and teachers
Before reading
Show the children examples of brass instruments. Online examples with audio
can be found at: http://ngfl.northumberland.gov.uk/music/orchestra/brass.htm
Can they name any of the instruments? How do they think the instruments are played?
Explain that an instrument is in the brass group when it is played by the player making their
lips buzz (or vibrate). Demonstrate if possible.

After reading
Encourage the children to make their own brass instrument. Get them to blow raspberry
sounds into a small plastic tube, such as a piece of hosepipe. The sound can be made
higher or lower by tightening or loosening the lips.

Extra information
The instruments shown on page 5 are: French horn (top left), trumpet (top right), didgeridoo
(centre), tuba (bottom right), and trombone (bottom left).
A didgeridoo and a conch shell might not look like brass instruments, but they are because
they have a mouthpiece, which you vibrate your lips into. Small brass instruments are high
sounding. Big brass instruments are low sounding because the air has further to travel.